WOLF SONNETS

Wolf Sonnets

R. P. LaRose

THE POETRY IMPRINT AT VÉHICULE PRESS

Published with the generous assistance of the Canada Council for the Arts and the Canada Book Fund of the Department of Canadian Heritage.

 Canada Council Conseil des arts
for the Arts du Canada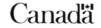

SIGNAL EDITIONS EDITOR: CARMINE STARNINO

Cover design by David Drummond
Photograph of the author by Erin Jade
Set in Minion by Simon Garamond
Printed by Livres Rapido Books

Dépôt légal, Library and Archives Canada and the
Bibliothèque national du Québec, fourth trimester 2022

LIBRARY AND ARCHIVES CANADA CATALOGUING IN PUBLICATION

Title: Wolf sonnets / R.P. Larose.
Names: LaRose, R. P., author.
Identifiers: Canadiana (print) 20220420076 | Canadiana (ebook)
20220420106 | ISBN 9781550656091
(softcover) | ISBN 9781550656152 (HTML)
Classification: LCC PS8623.A763635 W65 2022 | DDC C811/.6—dc23

Published by Véhicule Press, Montréal, Québec, Canada
www.vehiculepress.com

Distribution in Canada by LitDistCo
www.litdistco.ca

Distribution in the US by Independent Publishers Group
www.ipgbook.com

Printed in Canada on FSC certified paper.

For my grandfather, Paul LaRose

1

Not much rain, and a lot of wind.
Outer space for nobody thoughts.
You are made of four stars in four
colours, within the spiral heat
of galaxy. There is a word
for you in a language no one speaks.
My dreams are like whichever world
wind came from. Bloody mess, ill
intent. I have shelter and clothes
but not I. I have desire.
I have a car and change to give
and a room in a house with what
I want to love but not I. I
represent no one, so don't ask.

2

When I was child, a cyclone hit
the prairie. Hit my house, in fact.
Well, hit the kitchen, which was in
a mobile home on the waveless
sea, the last place you want to be.
Chairs hurled around in gusts of shouts
and spittle. My daddy shielded
from debris by his wild fortress
disappointment. The translations
of these childhood tornado gusts
offered by the psychologist
confuse me. Something. Something. Leave.
Grasses dance over the prairie,
fiercest in the fiercest storms, and
I grew up a little anxious.

3

Many nights, under the star pines
on my moss bed where, for 28
days, I lived alone, I heard wolves.
They howled down along the ravine
every odd night as the fire died.
Pups, moms, dads, uncles, grandparents,
everyone saying something, of course.
One day, four pups surrounded me
in silence. One tilted their head,
another bent their head down low.
Across the ravine, large shadows
moved through tamaracks like spruce smoke.

4

These wolf sonnets. Made by a fake.
Fake poems, fake book. Fake love, fake weight.
Make a home in this fake country.
Fake for the taking. Fake for free.
Tickets to every show you want.
Free land. Stolen the Christian way.
Give up your land rights. Script it.
I was born on this land. That was free
for an ancestor who gave up
something right. My great-great-grandfather
pleaded with a government:
"Dad always told me I'm Métis"
I plead: "My dad always told me."
We're never real enough for real.
We're never fake enough for fake.

5

To catch a trout, you need to move
like this, my father said. He left
me for the creek's meandered soul.
I took your calls during *Simpsons*
so I could feel I was only half
listening. Anyway, we joked.
We broke each other's heart-shaped masks
with another half-breathed phone call,
an episode of others' hopes
hinging on us not having hopes
of our own. Near the end of our
shows, we may think on each other,
I suppose. What parts of you I
loved, now I do without. Lucky
my father taught me how to fish.

6

Blue billows up an old TV
static made the same year blue wrapped
a tree. Billows like the ocean's
face, a trillion plastic bottles
tossed inside the maw. The sky too,
one day in ten thousand—the rest
are grey. But even though ribbons
strangle a forest by the trunks,
blue also is a bottled song
sent across the world by your friend
who misses you. He took in a
cold, crisp air and blew.

7

The big city, and no one here.
Not the grocer, not the millwright.
Dogs bark in the café. Bison
have returned. I think of all
the foam spilt on floors, taps running
like decimals, mis-brewed barrels,
and why we paid for empty pints.
Think of the moneyed mogul yachts
and jacked high schooler 4x4s
and, every bay, the schooner wakes.
It wasn't always the case. There
was a time before police.
Wolves, bison, woods, and each other
are packaged, wrapped, and on trend.

8

Today I mourn Chicago, lost
city of our last embrace. The
morning you left, streets under rain,
I became the last buffalo
my great-great-grandfather sparked
from sixteen ribs plucked in ashes.
My voice collected with the yard's
garbage, praying to the sun from
the top of a heap, I bought
a shirt and navy slim jacket
I still wear; those old emotions
on my rolled-up sleeves. On the fourth day,
we made love with fire, mud, and ash.
Later, we tried again with love.

9

The jar of strychnine made for wolves
killed Hélène Bouvette LaRose.
Her husband, the man they accused,
then fled with their son.
Past muskrats, moose, and buffalo.
Under new names: Boisvert, Greenwood.
Past the woods from whom we bleed,
toxic ponds and clear-cut borders—
boreal/prairie folk. Where men
murder boys over broken tires
and coffee shops murmur assent.
Lands in the middle of prairies.
I plucked from Buffalo Lake's jaws
broken glass thrown by my own blood's hand:
Great-great-grandfather—who, about
his mother's death, must have known something true.

10

Do not approach the suspects—8-
and-20-million white folk, deadly.
Don't approach the suspects lightly:
despite the rules and by the rules
police have chosen sides.
Broken tire? Don't ask that farmer.
Another white guy whose gun "went"
on automatic tangent.
Too soon to save us, the oil runs
out. After that will be the guns
deciding what we do: turn stork
and rave mad. Kill 'em all. The deals
I mean. The ones that gave us all
amber alerts blaring in the dark.

11

A civil arrangement of rose
messages, garnish, beaches, loose
speeches and the pit bull we cheered
on, that he would find his lovers
in sand. The try I thought could work
if we wanted. I searched your eyes-
that-seemed-to-be-searching-back for
what seemed a hundred pacific
waves against the dead chunks of wood
at the edge of California,
but you were looking at the colours
of my iris. I was dog whipped
flotsam, sand explosion, crater
blown, filled, blown, and salted water.

12

I found a pleasing calm one day
while walking in the wood, with loves,
not hearing any things they say,

my brain a drifting cloud of leaves,
a prayer made of birch and pine,
I was bluebirds, hawks, and grebes.

I'm so angry most of the time.
Your words are meaner than your mouth.
I watch those woods of speechless rhyme,

all the voices every new month
who are the songs of winglessly
soaring beings, the human uncouth.

The song: I've changed. I forgive me.
Its melody collapses, made
of shores, ebb, bay, devoid of end,
beginning, middle, like the sea.

13

A lake in woods. Eastern Slopes of
Western Rockies. Shallows so clear
brown beavers in the middle shine
to howls of wolves deeper in bush
than trees scraped of bark in bear tongue.
Rib bones ache with a needled nap,
afternoon of roots emerge
within a dream against my chest—
like the white wolf whose leaps so large
break pine and rotten logs like elk—
a Weyerhaeuser whip of ribbons
sips green red squirrel homes like tea.
Timber for the burbs. Enjoy your stay
in Mother's iridescent verse.

14

Sweet poet mill your miles of stone
against the nights we shook the earth
and burned our mornings to the bone.

All whom you love were at your birth.
You loved what you wanted of me:
the water poured a grimy bath:

the mulch, the meat, but not the tea.
My heart is like the art of math:
a love, a verb, an agency.

Then sweet poet lost her verse.
Like every smile I've never worn
of leaf and star, of sun and earth,

our only child was never born.
At night, in cold sea water June
birds live deeply in the ocean.
Blue whales dive toward the moon.

15

This working feeling that I know
we soon will talk again, tonight.
While writing poems in a journal,
I see myself drive off in tight
steel toes, long bucket, an apple,
coveralls, and a small photo
of you in my pocket. The bell.
Jobs. The money. The gears. The ride.
I come home. I put it all on
a table and seat. You arrive.
We make love last larger than this
world can hold, and we spill into
the only space minutes claim
that even work can't steal away.

16

A day for scarves and jackets—coats
with big fancy buttons. Rain clouds.
Multitudes of people gasping,
if you really think about it,
at the sky, green letters on blue
shifting through our fingers like wild
rice, the smell of lake mud.
We need to cleave the universe.
We need to quarry every thought.
A chance of fire. A chance of love.
Inside Café La Bicyclette
my name sits more gently than I
do as they ask a man to leave
because he eyes the ground and sighs.

17

The dancing orange fire's light
against the bank of Bluebell Creek
makes absolutely not a sense.
The antsy orange light of lamps,
underbelly smoke of our sky,
makes absolutely not a sound
while helping each one of us die
with what we should keep underground.
Letting go: the one thing I correctly do.
The evening wishes all the lamps
had known that things are better left
in dark. Moonlight deserves its
time with mountains, roads, and rooftops.

18

The view was so believable
humans had a way—knew the way—
of keep. Our home's become a plain
parents carry toddlers across.
There is no bush. My father cried
in elk linguistics. Words return
as woods across the old clear-cut
deep from outer space. People died.
There is no forest, only place.
How to survive: perceive the breadth
of love and time. Some other Earth
could have beautiful words for names.

19

Someone who may have been *a* one
I didn't say hello to, ask
the name of, say mine to, walked through
the deeper jungle of Khao Yai
by me wearing leech protection,
camo pants and—like me—reading
through glass the vines, ants, elephants,
and long-beaked phantoms. We neither
spoke a word more than a nod. It
was a long journey and we met
at the far point—the gegenschein
of the bush. The only someone
I've ever seen also alone
in a place so dear to me in
its distance from speech in all
my years of doing that. Walking
in the lands of woods. We'll never
know each other's second languages,
and our first has no words.

20

A field of fireflies in the sky
burned to gold the middle of night.
You told me of Georgia fields
even more gold and bright.
On the last day you saw me from
that ship within the wind, you said,
Don't cry. I drove my faded four
across the toxic vast America.
The border North to ride and dream
of all the things that last in me
from you; a sweater's worth you touched.
The being human dream inside
the middle of a snow storm's kiss
on the only day we ever
became cold Ithacans and thought,
Hmm, I'd miss this. Skimming purple
silhouettes on last night's highway
through Utah, I had all these thoughts
of Buffalo Lake, Ithaca,
and fireflies, Georgia.

21

More officially single now,
I more officially miss you.
Your gallery ally. Hired praise
of elemental floral beads.
A wait in the reeds of a call.
A gaze in all your paints. I love
forever what you've done despite
the bush of rose and weed and thorn.
I've never loved another like
the love I had for you. But I've
been better loved. And, yes, I've loved
better. We should have been the bay
of living trees where purple ferns
rapped the window. Artistic leaves
of eucalyptus in the grass.

22

When David Attenborough says:
"the negative impacts of human
actions on our Earth," what he ought
to mean is "the negative impacts
of colonial invasions
and Euro/American forced-
capitalist economies,
resource theft, and patriarchy
on ecosystems that had thrived
alongside and intertwined
with stewardship by Indigenous
peoples all across Mother Earth
since the beginnings of cosmos."

23

The window shakes the sill
from dream. The writhing jolt of poems
not yet printed from the belly
of the poet. No politics
except the political lives
we all live. Whenever Earth moves.
But write mundane things anyway
and depoliticize the page.
Or. Wreck these forests on the dole.
What words are we not speaking for?
When it is night, wind, leaves, I write:
we don't need glass to see the sky.

24

The world and its hurt take a rest
inside the wall of wet and safe
patter. Sleep pours its matter down
a fjord of forget and new touch.
Lens a focus on mouth, armpit
we feel in arms, droplets sliding
down. Though weapons line the pages
of the storm, don't bemoan the rains
before they drown to sleep the chords
of guns and shouting and the hordes.
They're mother's music finding us,
saying, It's OK to take this rest.
Little beings to earth from sky
splash and flail, but they never die.

25

Just there, THE MAPLE LEAF, by wind
appealed against, for its violence
and the songs people sing as one
from the heart to a genocide.
I'm tired of the goddamn coffee.
The colour of this TV screen
and the soundtracks to bloody sport.
The cheers and screams in melody.
The flags and their flagellations
of yet another not-empire
that calls itself a republic.
I'm not yet ready for the world's
first snowfall. Night, winter,
near the den, an old grey wolf knows.

26

The way the mid-air frog
forgets the tail they left in mud
when they wanted to feel grown. That
is how this loving feels. We have
the minutes of the sky, the space
where human beings, free, are fair.
One day dreamed between the nightlights.
No words for rich or less, this love
grows because our land is a home
that frog can safely fall toward.

27

You are cordially invited
to leave. Back to the beauties of
your mother, colossal Europe;
all the violence on her wares, all
the beauties of her wars. Pompeii.
Hints of moss in drops of whisky.
Feast on life as aperitifs
near cathedral executions.
I see you at the monuments
to murder, love, and poetry.
Nation to Nation, Earth to Earth,
concrete to rubble. When in Rome, as you
say. Except when you're roaming here
on Turtle Island. Funny that.

28

In all the million words for one
we need another study done
in language where the words for age
are beauty, wisdom, love, and rage.
No universal shape of pace—
no leaning gait of words called peace.
We all know that our bodies roil
in soft beginnings of the nights
before the dreams begin to boil
in this world of unequal rights.
I wished to quote Tranströmer, so
I fell asleep among shadows
and woke among wolves.

29

It's on the air, waves of matter—
what does, what doesn't, can and can't,
when down the curtain, all things fall
from the universe at once: there
is a new theory today that
moves us through walls faster than light
moves through an errant thought. We're told
to share all of our emotions.
Until we share our emotions.
Why not invent the words we need
for us, right now? Another name
for Earth's oeuvre is Blue Period.

30

Foucault beside the bed. Real
TV/pain loss. I regret not.
I regret us. I loved deeply
power. That we gave me. The you
of me. But who's the you of you?
And who is the me of me? I
know the floaty things in my eyes.
They can't see anything else. Paths
to loving and forgiveness are
to see us as the sleep we were
before the crumbling pines. And still
you fall asleep next to me. The
best poems are dense. They should be brief.

31

About the language no one speaks
because I can't speak the language
I wish I knew from childhood books:
instead I know this brutal off
german/roman master english
that seems real the reel seams the seams
reel the real seems. I love and
hate its lack of loving. Killing
birds with stones, et al. And though I'll
never know from birth the sweeter
words of Mother Earth, Michif,
I know that there's a language
here that no one knows but me.

32

The colours of moose, elk, muskrat,
and Nintendo. Hunting stories,
the bush, the chickens, the horses,
and *Star Trek*. Some friends across
a farmer's fields, loneliness, stars
but only of this galaxy,
and a hazy Andromeda.
A country school for country kids,
my beloved dog, my mom, dad,
and brother, how to hunt and fish
and live in a forest that is
now the beams of suburbs, somewhere.
Altogether somewhere elsewhere.

33

Some said Louis Riel was one
sixteenth of the lines of a poem
like a buffalo's rib is one
sixteenth of a buffalo's ribs.
Full mud buffalo rib. Like an
international space station
plucked from the beaches of the lake
tracing figure-eights, dancing star
in the sky it holds. Like this poem,
this book, this universe's view
of Buffalo Lake. Home. Also
one sixteenth of something whole, I guess.

The elevator snow's equal
fall on pine roofs and balconies
in this apartment in the woods.
Blue spruce homes and squirrel
at the window near your mattress
where the moon's brightly on the bear
in dreams you have as the endless
traffic sprawl of clubs through Jasper
and 109. The forests grieve.
Never take the woods at their words:
the aisles of meadows above
the miles of elk in rabid herds
galloping through the endless loss
empire corporations hide
beneath the timber's thick, bright moss.

35

For Hélène Bouvette LaRose

We grew ten timbers from the leaves
of Red River. I rode a mare
bank to bank, by borders and back,
chasing the hunter, loving pups.
They say he bought poison for wolves.
They say that he used it on me.
Together we had threaded beads
and weeds. Watched them grow. We believe
we bleed from the river's crevice;
I side with the wolves when their howls
deepen in the woods and rivers
for the violent, vacant father.
Now an ancestor, I ponder
my life, lost but loved, in dreams
of pups who never left my side
and nightmares of the one who did.

And suddenly your hands were on
my knees. The station left the train—
earth from people outward vanished
behind a blue sky where there were
no more stars but you were there. Six
years without our touch. A thousand
words and a thousand miles and no
change but that Dalat and this Milan
are the same city on the same day
when your hands first and now touch mine.
Things were never wrong for us, and
things were never right. How can a love
be so much like the northern sun?
Very hot—very bright—usually
on the other side of Earth.

37

The news this week is a letter
in a puzzle where the words are
languages no one has yet known.
It's week four of isolation,
recovery that doesn't move
in stasis, terrible news, white
washing everything.
A cough dryer than a dryer.
There is no such thing as cancel.
Pipelines will pump their hate until
the term *human resource* makes a
beeline for the sky and explodes.

38

Three tent villages erupted
Edmonton, erected by the
giving people here while
others drove by suv.
A poet I tell the image
who looks to me like poverty.
A poet I tell the image
who looks to me like wealth and greed.
WE ALL DESERVE CLOTHING.
WE ALL DESERVE SHELTER.
All the knights fasted and drained through
windows, feeling what cold is seen
in the rain—most merely near to.
Unpoliced Pekiwewin smoke
steals inside the burning cars.

39

I mean one night cleaving this bar
of light with one another caught
not knowing one day we'd be stopped
and turned around. We knew we were
going the bad directions but
deny, deny, deny despite
smelting all the rocks below the night.
Because what bells have they to say
the rights we never had, to say
that one's not enough without the other
I mean one night leaving this bar.

40

The local cluster ships our Earth
as island back toward the smell
of charcoal and thank you: the green
blades and petals licking up burned
barks and stumps. The sky is the ground
because we can't see border lines.
And when we gaze toward the hues
we already are the clouds, and
even looking down, feet complete
the gravel. It's an argument where one side
is correct and the other wrongs,
but *assuredly*, someone asserts,
there are two sides to truth.

41

Let fall the snow in angry swish
and rains cloud in drooped shoulder lumps.
Vets know the city's conscience;
watch cops in armoured vests harass
teenage sleepers on the bus
who rest quietly and breathe like us.
Yet fall snows in righteous wishes:
Who will be tomorrow's houseless?
Tell me how you feel about mean
breaths in the blood of powered men.
Autumn snow's relentless.
Land herself is taken aback.

42

Once, many many years ago,
I stirred a cup of air and spit
a newly thought of sweet and low
into a scary hollow pit.
The strength of numbers gathers us
first. Second: trauma. All of it.
Next: manmade and therefore too real.
Fall asleep with that empty cup,
where cup stands for "I can't do this"
and empty stands for "man enough."
Like all of us, I cry a little
every morning when I wake up.

43

Another blood-built neighbourhood
atop valleys of the rain where
houses hold to mud. We sing, stand
with shopping carts that line the banks
of creeks and corner malls. We wail.
Hold no say, no love, and no thanks
with the builders, priests, thieves, and cheats.
I've been told we are like a wolf,
den to den, pack to pack, moaning
to social solitude, a self
unrelated to the rest, alone.
I was made in someone else's home.
No matter what I write, I think
this should have been a love poem.

44

A younger man whose father loved
him strung them from the bearing post,
three thousand years before École
Polytechnique. Man camp Ilsa
Vista highway-of-our-tears white
celebrity serial box
masters of the Western canon:
Ulysses and Telemachus
murdered twelve for loving, living—
having no choice at all: Hello!
all those who own the *Odyssey*
but not the gendered murders that
were loudly praised and proudly done
by this beloved and only son.

45

What we want is a whole done
thing without a feel of finish.
My grandfather taught me to write
every road like my own driveway.
And I love my Zeus, with razor,
not because he cuts me quickly.
He gives me what I really want:
the jawline carved in poetry.
His ink blade shades away hours
from the contours of my day.
Close your eyes. Lean cool and wet mint
fingertips soft appraise the maw.
An edge edits, sawdust piles.
He's not yet done by miles.

46

What's out the bedroom window
looks inside.

Things howl out there,
and in bed underneath light movements,
a blanket roils.

We move uniformly entangled from window
to window in the moon prairie mountain foothills,

a milk landscape where
we shutter the doors and screens
that utter against us.

Our house a body of woods
pulled like teeth from the children
and their perfectly possible futures
underneath the house, not far away.

47

Seeds glow on the crystals plain
and to the big eyes, so do I.
In my subnivean
I dream of the blood above
in the breath of all forms of mean.

To run each day and never travel far
I must be as silent as the big eyes' seamless flight—
a patch that flits but never flickers
through paths in flake stars.

Above the crust sky stars screech
as they divulge a presence
on a branch earing me.

My pulse drums upward to a sink of sound.

A catching face.

Memory, please stay near.

If I remember they are there—
If I never move—
I'll be here.

Fiddle splat across the pages
of the forest, read clean by wolves.
Always everything by wolves. Like
1880, the year mom died.
All the basic numbers are names.
Counting, an easy way to blame.
Night close, another wasted day
when I was asked to be in control.
All attempts crumble from the tips
of rain-wet fingers.
There can never be eight wolves. There
can only ever be something
we call eight wolves.

ACKNOWLEDGEMENTS

Some of these poems ("13" "19" "46" and "47") have appeared in *The Walrus* or in the chapbook *A Dream in the Bush* by Anstruther Press with altered shapes, phrases, and titles. Many sincere thanks to the editors and teams of those publications.

Thank you to Bes Mehari, Denise Roa, Sang Beom Seo, and Debra Wong for help with "40" and for listening to me talk about the manuscript between rallies. Thank you also to Idman Omar for help with several poems in the manuscript and for the great talks.

Thank you to Noochy Phatchanee Pliankoed, Sang Beom Seo, Honoka Takei, Natani Notah, Renia White, Kyrie Ransom, and Victoria Halcrow—those who have taught me so much about love, friendship, poetry, and better ways of being. All of you are in these poems, and I love you very much.

A special thank you to Victoria Halcrow for the gift of the book's title.

Thank you to my childhood and to-this-day friends, Graeme, Dan, Kevin, Dustin, Tara-Lee, Tara, and Jill.

To everyone—staff, cohort, students, and professors—who helped me through the Cornell University MFA, my thanks. A very special thank you to Michael Prior for requesting to share my poems. Thank you to Ishion Hutchinson, Lyrae Van Clief-Stefanon, Jolene Rickard, Carol Warrior, and Alice Fulton for the thoughtful, brilliant teachings and support.

Wolf Sonnets would not be wolf sonnets without certain excellent mentors at the University of Alberta. Marilyn Dumont, Bert Almon, and Derek Walcott—you will be forever in my heart and poems. Thank you also to Thomas Wharton and Christine Wiesenthal for excellent teachings in narrative.

My love and appreciation for the "Walcott Eight." I learned so much from you all, and I'll never forget our weeks writing sonnets in St. Lucia under Derek's instruction.

Thank you to Carmine Starnino for the patience, encouragement, and brilliant insights into the manuscript. Thank you to everyone at Véhicule Press.

Thank you also to the instructors in grade school who supported my creativity and tolerated my eccentricities: Lotoski, Schollie, Gregory, and Clark.

Thank you to Mom, Dad, Little Brother, Grandpa Paul, and all my friends and family.

Talya Rubin • Richard Sanger • Stephen Scobie
Peter Dale Scott • Deena Kara Shaffer
Carmine Starnino • Andrew Steinmetz • David Solway
Ricardo Sternberg • Shannon Stewart
Philip Stratford, trans. • Matthew Sweeney
Harry Thurston • Rhea Tregebov • Peter Van Toorn
Patrick Warner • Derek Webster • Anne Wilkinson
Donald Winkler, trans. • Shoshanna Wingate
Christopher Wiseman • Catriona Wright
Terence Young